ODYSSEUS AND THE WOODEN HORSE OF TROY

from Homer's *Iliad*
retold by Martin Waddell

ODYSSEUS

AGAMEMNON

ACHILLES

HECTOR

HELEN

PARIS

PATROCLUS

PART I

There was once a great war between the Greeks and the Trojans. It lasted ten years but the Greeks won in the end by using their brains … and a huge wooden horse.

It started when Helen, the beautiful wife of the Greek king, was stolen from him by Paris, the son of the king of Troy.

"This means war!" vowed the Greek king.

The Greeks gathered a huge army and a fleet of ships to sail against Troy. The king's brother, Agamemnon, was in command … but the wisest of all the Greek heroes didn't join in.

"We need our hero Odysseus," decided the Greeks, and they sent a messenger to fetch him.

"He's gone raving mad," the messenger was told. "He can't go to war. He's out in the fields now, sowing salt. No one sows salt in a field! And he's got a giant ox and a small ass pulling his plough. Can you imagine that? An ox and an ass yoked together. He's crazy!"

"Let's see how mad Odysseus really is!" the messenger said to himself, and he laid Odysseus' baby son in the path of the plough.

"If he cuts his son in half with the plough, then I'll go back and tell Agamemnon he's off his head," the messenger decided. "If he doesn't … then he's not mad."

Of course, Odysseus didn't cut his son in half.

"You're not mad," the messenger told him. "You made us all take an oath to protect Helen, long before she married our king. If anyone harmed her, you said, we'd all band together to protect her. Now someone has harmed her … and you're trying to get out of it."

"The idea was to stop us fighting amongst ourselves about who should have Helen," Odysseus said. "It had nothing to do with going to war with the Trojans!"

"That sounds a pretty weak excuse to me," the messenger said. "I don't know why people call you a hero, if the first thing you do when there is trouble is run away!"

Odysseus had to join in … but he didn't like it. The Greek warriors were boasting that they would take Troy and save Helen and be back home before breakfast.

"Taking the city of Troy is not going to be easy," Odysseus warned them. "The Trojan king is a wise ruler, and he has many friends who will join in on his side. His son Hector is one of the greatest warriors there's ever been and …"

"Now he's scared of Hector!" some of the Greeks muttered. "Some hero!"

"We've got Achilles on our side!" they told Odysseus. "He's a *real* hero. Achilles is a match for Hector any day!"

"Where *is* Achilles then?" asked Odysseus. "I don't see him."

"He's around *somewhere*," the Greeks said, but then they found out that he wasn't.

Some Greeks said that Achilles' mother was one of the gods, and she knew that he would be killed in front of the walls of Troy, so she had sent him away where no one could find him.

"That can't be true," some others said. "Achilles was blessed by the gods. His mother dipped him in the River Styx when he was a baby. Everyone knows he can't be killed or wounded in battle."

They kept arguing about it, hoping that Achilles would turn up, but he didn't.

"Who needs Achilles? We're Greeks. We'll win anyway!" the Greeks decided.

"No, no we won't!" said one of their soothsayers. "We can't beat the Trojans without Achilles. I *know*, because the gods have given me the gift of being able to tell the future. No Achilles … and we don't take Troy." Everyone believed the soothsayer. They believed in their gods, and if the gods had given the soothsayer the power to see the future, then the soothsayer must be right.

"*You* get Achilles for us!" Agamemnon ordered Odysseus. "You have to. We need him."

Odysseus sent spies everywhere, and at last word came back: "Achilles is at the court of King Lycomedes. He's disguised himself as one of the king's daughters."

"Achilles, dressed up as a woman!" Agamemnon laughed. "There can't be many women there who look like Greek heroes!"

"There'll be hundreds of women, all heavily veiled. I can't go round asking them to show me their faces, can I?" Odysseus said. "If I started to ask them, I wouldn't find him anyway. He's not going to wait for me to find him. He'll be off somewhere else."

"Achilles is not going to get himself dragged into a war taking *your* orders," is what Odysseus was really thinking, but he didn't say that to the Commander-in-Chief.

"I'm in charge of this war," Agamemnon replied. "I give orders to *so-called* heroes like you … and *I'm* ordering *you* to fetch Achilles. Now go and do it!"

Odysseus didn't like taking orders from Agamemnon, but he
knew he had to come up with something to save his reputation.

"If Achilles can disguise himself, so can I," he decided, and he
dressed himself up as a merchant.

He went to the court with lots of perfumes and jewels and
beautiful clothes to sell … and some weapons.

The women started testing the perfume, and trying on the jewels
and feeling the beautiful clothes … all but one woman. *She* was
only interested in trying out the weapons, to see how they would
feel if *she* had to use them in battle.

Odysseus tapped *her* on the shoulder.

"You're coming with me," he told Achilles.

"I don't want to go," said Achilles.

"Neither do I," said Odysseus. "We both know that it doesn't make sense to wage a long and bloody war with the Trojans to get Helen back. But Agamemnon has spoken. He's our Commander-in-Chief, and we're both Greeks … we have no choice."

"I was told I'd find glory if I went to Troy, but I'd have a short life if I did," argued Achilles.

"But we need you!" said Odysseus, and in the end Achilles gave in.

"Achilles is back. Troy will fall!" thought the Greeks and they sailed for Troy in their great fleet with their huge army and all their weapons of war.

PART II

Odysseus had been right when he said it would take the Greeks a long time to conquer Troy. Nine years went by, and the city was still under siege, with the Greeks camped before it, but they couldn't break their way in through the walls. They had swords and armour and slingshots and arrows and spears and lances and daggers and huge rock-throwing machines to help them.

It wasn't a war as war would be now, fought with tanks and guns and rockets. In some ways it was more terrible, for the Greeks and the Trojans often fought man to man, face to face, sometimes with the blood dripping from their bare hands as they tore at each other. Sometimes the Greeks won a day's fighting, sometimes the Trojans did.

The Greeks began to argue amongst themselves and some of them felt that the gods had turned against them.

The worst row of all was between Achilles and Agamemnon …
which didn't surprise Odysseus one bit. Achilles was doing most of the
fighting in a war he'd never wanted to fight in the first place, and the
Commander-in-Chief was giving all the orders. Achilles was looking for
an excuse to withdraw from the
struggle, and he found one.

Achilles' chance came after
a Greek victory when
Agamemnon took the captured
daughter of a High Priest of
Apollo to be his slave. The
priest came to Agamemnon
and begged for the release of
his daughter.

"No!" said Agamemnon, rudely refusing the High Priest.

Soon after that, a great sickness spread through the Greek camp
and the War Council met to discuss what had gone wrong.

"Agamemnon has angered Apollo by insulting his priest!" Achilles
told the Council. "You can't insult the gods and hope to win battles.
Apollo has sent this sickness amongst us because of Agamemnon.
He must return the girl to her father."

"Let Achilles give me *his* favourite slave in exchange. If he does
that, I'll give *my* slave back to the priest," Agamemnon replied,
thinking fast.

"I *won* my slave by winning your battles for you!" Achilles shouted back, losing his temper. "Why should I lose her?"

"Because *I* give the orders around here!" said Agamemnon and the War Council agreed.

"Then you can fight your war without me!" said Achilles, and he stormed out of the tent.

"He'll cool down later and come back," thought the Greeks, but Achilles had no intention of coming back. He began making preparations to sail home.

The soothsayer had told the Greeks that they couldn't conquer the Trojans without Achilles' help … and so it seemed to be.

They lost battle after battle, and were driven back from the walls of the city behind a great defensive barrier they had built to protect their ships. The Greeks who had come to besiege Troy now found themselves besieged, with their backs to the sea. If their ships were taken, they knew they would be slaughtered.

Achilles watched the battle from his tent.

He saw a wounded man being rescued from the battlefield by a Greek.

"I can't go down there, after all I have said," Achilles told his friend Patroclus. "But I'm worried in case someone I know has been wounded. Could you find out who got hurt?"

Patroclus did as he was asked but while he was there the Greeks asked him to persuade Achilles to return to the battle.

"Achilles is a great warrior," they told Patroclus. "But you are older and wiser than he is. Before you came here, your father told you to look after Achilles, and guide him to do what is right. Guide him now! We need him to fight."

"Achilles won't fight," said Patroclus.

"Well … if he won't fight himself, ask him to lend you his armour, and some of his men," the Greeks said. "You know that the Trojans fear Achilles more than anyone else in our army. Even if they only *believe* he has come back it will help us."

"But I'll be wearing the armour, not Achilles," a puzzled Patroclus said.

"The Trojans won't know it is you," the Greeks explained. "If they see the gleaming armour the gods are supposed to have made for Achilles, they'll think that you *are* Achilles … especially if you come into the battle with his men around you."

Meanwhile Trojans had broken through the defences, bringing torches with them to set fire to the ships, which would cut off the Greeks' last hope of escape.

Just at that moment, what must have seemed like a miracle happened to save the Greeks.

They saw a group of men charging into the battle, led by a man in glittering armour.

They knew it must be Achilles … who else could it be? They knew, and so did the Trojans. Everyone believed that Achilles was blessed by the gods, and could never be killed in battle.

The Greeks fought back fiercely, inspired by their hero, and the Trojans were forced to retreat in confusion, towards Troy.

They were streaming away from the fight, blood-spattered and wounded and beaten, when *their* hero, Hector, galloped into the battle on his war chariot … heading straight for the man in the gleaming armour.

A stone struck the Trojan who was driving the chariot, and he fell off and lay on the ground senseless.

Hector leapt down to defend his fallen friend, and two other Trojans joined him.

The so-called Achilles in the gleaming armour found himself facing them alone, one against three. The Trojans closed in on Achilles. A blow to the head stunned him, and he dropped his shield. As Hector's spear pierced his armour, another Trojan stabbed him in the back.

The Greeks thought Achilles was dead … but everyone soon saw that the man who lay dead wasn't Achilles!

"Achilles refused to fight," said the Greeks bitterly. "Our *great* hero stayed in his tent and let his brave friend Patroclus die in his place."

Achilles was ashamed, and his shame turned to hate against Hector. His longing for revenge overcame his fear of the glorious death that had been foretold for him if he went to Troy.

"I will kill the man who killed my friend!" he roared.

With the *real* Achilles back to fight furiously on their side, no one could withstand the Greeks. They attacked their enemies, stabbing and killing, forcing the Trojans back to the gates of their own besieged city.

The Trojan king, Priam, opened the gates of the city when he saw that his son Hector's men were all being killed.

The Trojans poured in … but Hector stayed outside, alone, despairing over the deaths of so many of his friends, men that he had led for long years in the war with the Greeks over Helen.

"Come inside, my son," the king pleaded. "Achilles has vowed he will kill you himself. The gods are on his side. No one can withstand Achilles. If you stay where you are you will die."

"My men fought many enemies for me," Hector replied. "How can I refuse battle with one man alone, even if that man is Achilles?"

King Priam went on pleading and weeping … but Hector stayed outside the gates.

Achilles came, burning with hate and the need for revenge.

Like everyone else, Trojan or Greek, Hector believed he would die at the hands of the raging Achilles. It was too late now to try to make peace.

If he stood and fought, he would die … he did not want to die so he tried to escape … but he couldn't.

On one side of Hector lay the Greek army. On the other were the great closed gates of his father's city of Troy. Achilles now stood between him and the gates, barring his way to the city.

Hector found himself despairingly circling the city, trying to find a way in. Every time he moved close to the walls, Achilles was there first, waiting and ready to kill him.

Then Hector surprised everyone. He came out into the open, and moved toward Achilles. He called out the name of one of his brothers, as though his brother was *there* by his side, and would help him to fight Achilles.

"He's gone mad with despair and sorrow, and fear of Achilles!" thought the Greeks, and maybe he had, with the fate of so many men on his mind, friends that he'd led to their deaths in the war with the Greeks.

"One of the gods must have taken the form of his brother, and come to help him in the fight," the Trojans decided. "Either that, or he's seeing someone who just isn't there."

19

Hector threw his spear at Achilles, but it bounced off the Greek's shield and fell to the ground. Then Hector looked wildly round, calling the name of his brother … but no one was there.

The Trojan turned back, and he made a last desperate charge at Achilles. Hector fell with the great warrior's spear thrust deep in his neck, before he could get near enough to Achilles to fight.

The dying Hector pleaded with Achilles to return his body to the king of Troy.

"The dogs will have your body!" Achilles swore angrily, spitting in Hector's blood-spattered face.

He tied Hector's ankles to his war chariot, and drove round the walls of Troy, dragging the dead body behind him, scraping and bouncing and bumping on the dusty ground. Achilles did it several times, and he came back later on, and did it again. It was a brutal revenge for the death of his friend … but still Troy hadn't fallen.

PART III

A truce was arranged, after the Trojan king had pleaded with Achilles for the return of his son's body for burial.

"Suppose we let you marry our king's daughter," a Trojan suggested to Achilles, during the truce. "If we do that, would you talk to the Greeks and try to make peace?"

"Perhaps I can put an end to this stupid war now," Achilles thought to himself. He went to the Temple of Apollo to talk about the marriage … he was going to his death, although he didn't know it.

Paris, the Trojan king's son who had started the war in the first place by stealing Helen, wanted to avenge the death of his brother Hector. He fired a poisoned arrow at Achilles. It struck him in the heel, and Achilles died from the wound. He had won what the Greeks called glory by winning his battles, but he died before Troy, as his mother had told him he would.

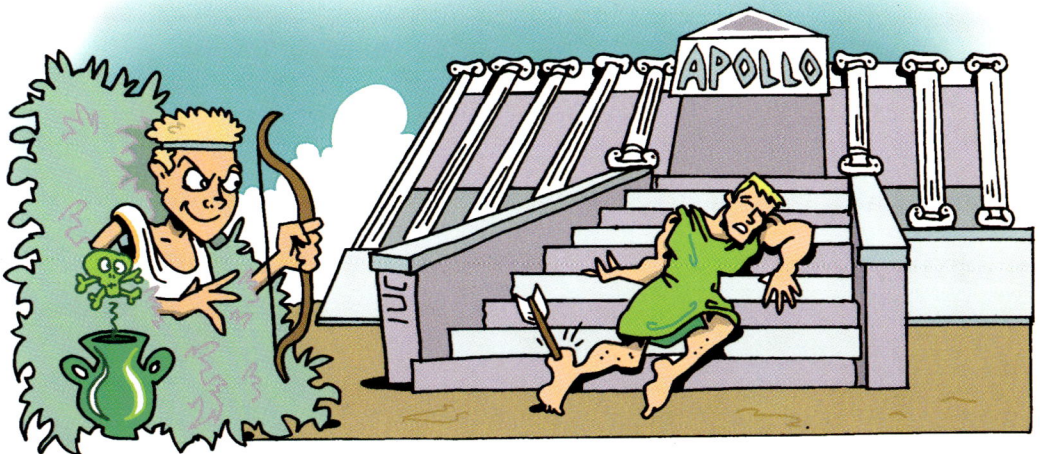

"Achilles was blessed by the gods. He *couldn't* die from a wound in the heel," the Greeks told themselves, when they first heard the news. They couldn't believe it was true.

But Achilles was dead. They couldn't argue with that.

"His mother must have held him up by the heel, when he was dipped in the River Styx," they decided. "That's why he died from the wound. The arrow struck his heel just where her hand held him, so that bit of his body was left unprotected."

Achilles was dead, but the war still dragged on and on. Greek killed Trojan and Trojan killed Greek, and Troy was still besieged, but couldn't be taken.

And then Paris was killed. His death was important, in a way that few people understood at the time, Trojan or Greek … but one of the few who understood was Odysseus.

"Helen had no choice when she left our king. The gods had blessed Paris so that no woman could resist him," the Greeks had been told, before they went to war to save Helen. Perhaps they believed it was true, and perhaps *she* believed it as well. However it was, when Paris died, Helen decided that she loved the Greek king again, and wanted to go back to her husband.

"For that to happen, Troy must fall first," she decided, and she sent word to Odysseus by using the spies he had inside the city.

Now Odysseus had Helen as an ally inside Troy's walls, as well as his spies. He knew that Helen had friends who would help her in Troy, but she had enemies too. Many Trojans blamed her for the trouble her beauty had caused.

First Helen's friends helped Odysseus steal a statue of the goddess Athena from inside the city. It was believed that Troy would fall if the statue ever left the city … but Troy's walls didn't fall.

"That wasn't much use!" thought the Greeks.

Odysseus said nothing. He knew that taking the statue would fit his plans well.

"Agamemnon has fought many battles, and Troy's walls are still standing," Odysseus told the War Council. "Let's try it *my* way for a change. We'll see if cunning can win us the city, where all Agamemnon's fighting has failed."

The Greeks stopped fighting, and started packing up, as though they were going somewhere.

"Ten years of war, and they've suddenly stopped?" the Trojans said to themselves. "What's this about?"

All the tents were taken away, along with the war chariots and the siege weapons. The Greeks began preparing their ships for a long voyage.

Then the Greeks started building an immense wooden figure, shaped like a horse. It was so big that it reached the top of the city wall.

"What's that supposed to be?" thought the Trojans. Some of them believed it was a gift for the gods, and others thought it was a new weapon they'd not seen before.

The Trojan king sent spies to find out.

"We angered the goddess Athena by stealing her statue," the spies were told. "The horse is a gift to turn her anger aside. We're leaving it here as a tribute to the goddess."

"That *could* be true," thought the Trojans. "They did steal our statue."

"And the goddess *was* angry!" others said. "She has ordered the Greeks to go away from Troy."

The next day the Greeks sailed away, leaving the huge wooden horse. The Trojans waited for a while to see if the Greeks would come back, but they didn't.

The Trojans came out of the city to look at the huge wooden horse.

"It would look good in the city, if we brought it in," some of them said. "It's a trophy of war, a gift left for us by the Greeks." They started discussing how to get the huge horse in through Troy's gates.

"What madness is this?" said the High Priest Laocoon. "Have you not learned enough to know that we can't trust the Greeks? For my part, I fear the Greeks most when they offer gifts."

Laocoon threw his lance at the wooden horse. When the lance struck the side of the horse, there was a hollow sound, like a groan.

"If it's hollow, there could be something inside," some Trojans said.

"So it's hollow. What does that prove?" others asked.

Then a Greek prisoner was dragged through the crowd. He had been badly beaten and was quivering with fear.

"This man is named Sinon," the Trojans who'd found him explained. "He claims Odysseus hates him and left him here to face certain death at our hands."

"We'll spare your life if you tell us the truth about the huge horse," the Trojan leaders told Sinon.

At first Sinon seemed too scared to speak, but then he said, "The horse is a gift that we left for the goddess Athena. A soothsayer warned us that if you got the horse into Troy we would get beaten if we ever fought you again. That's why we made it so huge."

Some of the Trojans believed what he said, and some didn't. They were still arguing about it when a rumour spread through the crowd. "Laocoon the High Priest is dead! The way that he spoke of the horse angered the gods. Two foul serpents were sent from the depths of the sea. The two serpents coiled their slimy bodies around Laocoon's sons. Laocoon fought to save them and failed. He died in the serpents' coils."

Sure enough, Laocoon and his sons lay dead on the shore.

No one seemed to doubt the story of how he had died. They believed that Laocoon had been wrong all along, and that he had angered the gods. It was what they wanted to hear.

Somehow the Trojans moved the huge wooden horse into Troy. They opened the gates wide and all the people pushed and hauled it. They believed they had to do it to please the gods, no matter how big the horse was.

Everyone was excited and filled with the glory of winning the war.

They had a great celebration, and when it was over they all went to bed, and they slept.

The huge wooden horse stood in the darkness of the sleeping city, towering over the rooftops.

As Troy slept, the Greek ships came back, and the Greeks landed. They surrounded the city of Troy and they waited.

No one saw Sinon as he crept towards the horse. He tapped on the side of the horse, and someone tapped back. A trapdoor opened, and out came the Greeks who'd been hiding inside.

The guards at the gates were overpowered by the small band of Greeks helped by Helen's friends. The guards died, and that left the city defenceless.

Sinon opened the gates, and the Greeks outside charged into the city. They pillaged and burned the great city of Troy. The Trojan king died with the rest of his men.

Helen was returned to her husband without one hair on her beautiful head being harmed.

It worked out just as Odysseus had planned.

The war that had begun when Helen was stolen by Paris ended with bloodshed and burning and looting and the screams of men dying in pain, the way all wars do. But it wasn't the sharp swords and spears of the Greeks or their terrible arrows or their great rock-throwing machines that won the war for the Greeks. It wasn't their heroes who died in the fight, or the others who lived to fight many more battles.

It was the cunning of Odysseus that conquered the Trojans and brought down the city of Troy … with the help of a huge wooden horse.